The Heartbeat Drum

THE HEARTBEAT DRUM

The Story of Carol Powder, Cree Drummer and Activist

written by **Deidre Havrelock**

illustrated by **Aphelandra**

Abrams Books for Young Readers

New York

Deep in the woods, in a log cabin facing a lake,
a family lived . . .
        hunting . . .
            fishing . . .
                and making music.

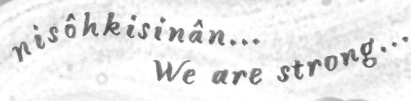

nisôhkisinân...
We are strong...

Moshum's drumbeat went,
PUH-POM, PUH-POM, PUH-POM, PUH-POM.
Uncles' voices poured out,
"Hi-ya, hi-ya, way-ah, hey-ah-oh."

Kokum sang,
"We are strong . . .
We are singing . . .
And we will continue."

ninikamonân...
We are singing...

Whenever Carol
sang along to her
family's music,
her heart was light
and full of joy.

mîna nika-âhkamêyimonân...
And we will continue...

One day, Moshum told Carol,
"Women first made the drum.
It is the sound of a mother's heartbeat,
and now you must learn to drum
so that our music can continue."

Moshum made Carol her
own hand drum—
just like his, only smaller.

She couldn't wait
to hear her drum
but first it had to dry
so that the moose hide
could shrink tight.

When Moshum finally brought Carol
her beautiful new drum and a drumstick made
from a willow branch, he sat her down.

"Creator has shown me something," he said.
"You are gifted with song, and in the future,
you will become a singer."
"Me?" Carol asked.

"Yes, *you*," he said. "But understand what I have seen.
When I am gone and you grow older,
our ways will change—women will not be accepted.
You are going to help bring women back to the drum
because that is where they belong, beside us.
Children belong there, too.

"Why?" asked Carol.

"Because that's the only time anyone's going to heal,"
replied Moshum.

Carol thought about how Moshum's music made her feel. She imagined herself spreading healing through her own songs and through the heartbeat of her own special drum. She couldn't wait to become a singer, so she hit her new drum in agreement—POM!

Carol trained with Moshum's drumming group.
They drummed at home, at ceremonies, and especially
at powwows, using a big drum called *Grandfather Drum*.
Even though the drum was giant like Moshum,
its heartbeat still came from a mother.

nisôhkisinân...
We are strong...

ninikamonân...
We are singing...

Their drumbeat went,
PUH-POM, PUH-POM, PUH-POM, PUH-POM.
Their voices poured out,
"Hi-ya, hi-ya, way-ah, hey-ah-oh."
Their words sang,
"We are strong . . .
We are singing . . .
And we will continue."

mîna nika-âhkamêyimonân...
And we will continue...

But every year, Moshum's drumming became
a little bit lighter, and his walking a little bit slower.
Until one evening, Carol was called to his bedside.

Moshum said to her,
"Granddaughter, today I am going to the next world.
Remember everything I taught you. Remember your gift."

Carol's heart beat with sadness . . .
PUH-POM, PUH-POM . . .
as she promised to practice her drum
without Moshum.

Carol kept her promise.
She practiced . . .
PUH-POM, PUH-POM . . .

and practiced . . .
PA-PUM, PA-PUM . . .

and practiced . . .
PUM-PUM-PUM!

Eventually, Carol became a mother.
She made drums for her children
so that her family's music could continue.
"Listen to the heartbeat of the drum,"
she told her children, just like Moshum taught her.

After many years, Carol missed drumming at powwows,
so she formed a female drumming group called Chubby Cree.
She taught the women her songs and how to drum.

But when Carol and her group arrived at a powwow,
things had changed just like Moshum had warned.
No other women were sitting at the drum.
And instead of welcoming words, Carol heard,

"It is not tradition for women to hit the drum."
"If women hit the drum, they will kill the drum's spirit!"

But Carol knew the men's words weren't true.
She knew women gave life to the drum.
And she understood that it was time to speak up.

At first, Carol was scared of being in front of people,
having to speak her truth about why she was drumming . . .
What would people think? Would they laugh at her?
Would they call her disrespectful?

"I want to educate my people about women drumming,"
she called out to the crowd one day after being turned away
at a powwow. As she spoke, her heart beat with nervousness . . .
PA-PUM! PA-PUM! PA-PUM!

It seemed like nobody wanted to listen.

But Carol didn't give up.

She continued . . . by teaching and speaking out about the importance of honoring women— even when they are at the drum.

And as grandchildren were born,
she continued by passing on Moshum's teachings
to the next generation.

Today, despite those who disagree,
Carol and her group share their music at
climate events for the healing of Mother Earth.
They sing and drum at special ceremonies
honoring residential school survivors.
And they pour their healing music over
all those who have lost loved ones.

Sometimes they simply meet in the park, playing for anyone who needs to feel the joy of a mother's heartbeat.

ninikamonân...
We are singing...

Their drumbeat goes,
PUH-POM, PUH-POM, PUH-POM, PUH-POM.

Their voices pour out,
"Hi-ya, hi-ya, way-ah, hey-ah-oh."

Their words sing,
"We are strong . . .
We are singing . . .
And we will continue."

mîna nika-âhkamêyimonân...
And we will continue...

AUTHOR'S NOTE

Carol Powder grew up in Sandy Beach, Alberta. She lived with her great-grandparents, grandparents, aunts and uncles, and her mother and siblings in one-room log cabins built by hand and insulated with mud and grass. It was her grandmother, Louisa Powder, who sang the song in this book: "nisôhkisinân, ninikamonân, mîna nika-âhkamêyimonân."

These Plains Cree words mean, "We are strong. We are singing. And we will continue." Below is the song written in Cree syllabics:

ᓂᐢᐦᑭᓯᐋᐤ ᓂᓂᑲᒧᐋᐤ ᒥᓇ ᓂᑲ ᐊᐦᑲ�7ᐱᒧᐋᐤ

It was Carol's great-grandfather, Harry Powder, who told her she would bring women back to the drum. Carol started a drumming group in 2011. In 2016, she named the group Chubby Cree after her deceased and much-loved younger brother, Rick, whose nickname was "Chubby Cree." She did not know her female drumming group would stir up so much controversy because when she was a child, she saw lots of girls learning to drum. But over time, girls were increasingly kept from the drum due to colonialism and the residential school teaching that men held authority over women. In many Indigenous cultures, women are honored as powerful because Creator gave them the power to create life. Unfortunately, today this power is sometimes seen as a dangerous quality. But the power of women is positive—women and girls bring life and joy!

Carol taught all nine of her children to sing and drum, and then she taught her grandchildren. Her grandson Noah Green took to the drum with passion. He has been drumming and singing with Carol in public since he was two. On October 18, 2019, at the age of eight, Noah Green sang and drummed at the Edmonton Climate Strike alongside climate activist Greta Thunberg. Today, Carol and Noah live in Edmonton, Alberta, Canada, where they travel extensively as Chubby Cree, bringing healing music wherever they go.

ILLUSTRATOR'S NOTE

In the summer of 2022, I traveled to Oneida, Wisconsin, to attend the 48th Annual Oneida Pow Wow. It was my first powwow, and I didn't know what to expect, but I did know the trip would help me illustrate this book better—and give me a new opportunity to connect with my heritage as a descendant of the Oneida Nation.

At the powwow, I saw a few groups of drummers, each sitting in a circle around a huge drum, just like how Carol sat with Moshum at the Grandfather Drum. I stood as close as possible to take in every little detail. Little did I know that I would not simply observe the performance but *feel* it.

Drumming is not only a beautiful art form, but also a full-body experience—both for the drummer and the listener. The sounds of the drummers' voices and the beat of the drum reverberated all around and through the crowd. At that moment, I really felt the drum like it was a heartbeat. And I imagined a mother watching over all of us, proud that the tradition of the drum was continuing onward.

In this book, I have attempted to translate the sounds and feelings I experienced that day into visual art. When you see my illustrations of Carol beating her drum with joy and determination and purpose, I hope you feel those same emotions echoing in your own heart.

A NOTE FROM CAROL POWDER

Working on this book with Deidre has stirred up so many good memories. I've always carried in my heart that memory of me sitting under the tree with Moshum, and now to know that it is in a book is amazing. I never thought of my life being in a book, but now my grandkids can look back and read the story of why we drum. They can look back and see their Ancestors and know how loving and kind and musical our family was. I see this book as an opportunity for everyone to learn about the way in which I was taught.

kinanāskomitin nimosōm kahkiyaw
kīkwaya kā-kiskinwahamawiyan ēkwa kā-wāpahtēhiyan.
kinanāskomitin kākikē.

Photo by Alexandra Jarrett.

◄ Carol Powder with young members of Chubby Cree, including Noah, Elija, and Octavious.

For the many much-loved children, grandchildren, and great-grandchildren of Carol Powder, so their music may continue. —D.H.

For the three teachers who influenced my life the most:
Tanya Cochran, Chris Blake, and Mark Robison. Thank you. —A.

The artwork for this book was painted digitally,
with some details rendered in ink with a brush pen.

The text of this book is set in Garalda and hand-lettered by the artist.

Cataloging-in-Publication Data has been applied for and
may be obtained from the Library of Congress.

ISBN 978-1-4197-5668-9

Text © 2024 Deidre Havrelock
Illustrations © 2024 Aphelandra
Book design by Andrea Miller and Aphelandra
Cree translation by maskwacām Consulting

Printed and bound in China
10 9 8 7 6 5 4 3 2 1

Abrams Books for Young Readers are available at special discounts
when purchased in quantity for premiums and promotions as well as fundraising
or educational use. Special editions can also be created to specification.
For details, contact specialsales@abramsbooks.com or the address below.

Abrams® is a registered trademark of Harry N. Abrams, Inc.

ABRAMS The Art of Books
195 Broadway, New York, NY 10007
abramsbooks.com